About the Author

A young adult, artist, painter, designer and educator, Chifa Gatri, born in Lausanne, Switzerland, enjoys writing poems, painting songs, discovering cultures, and the company of plants and animals. Her days are spent in a quite paradise-like village in the canton of Vaud between nature, neighbours, festivals and meditation. She travelled to many countries and lived in three of them. The first time author studied, worked, fell in love with art, and wrote about things and people and other realms.

Some Kind of Bridges Leading to Oneself

Chifa Gatri

Some Kind of Bridges Leading to Oneself

Olympia Publishers
London

www.olympiapublishers.com
OLYMPIA PAPERBACK EDITION

Copyright © Chifa Gatri 2024

The right of Chifa Gatri to be identified as author of
this work has been asserted in accordance with sections 77 and 78 of
the Copyright, Designs and Patents Act 1988.

All Rights Reserved

No reproduction, copy or transmission of this publication
may be made without written permission.
No paragraph of this publication may be reproduced,
copied or transmitted save with the written permission of the publisher,
or in accordance with the provisions
of the Copyright Act 1956 (as amended).

Any person who commits any unauthorised act in relation to
this publication may be liable to criminal
prosecution and civil claims for damage.

A CIP catalogue record for this title is
available from the British Library.

ISBN: 978-1-80439-238-6

This is a work of fiction.
Names, characters, places and incidents originate from the writer's
imagination. Any resemblance to actual persons, living or dead, is
purely coincidental.

First Published in 2024

Olympia Publishers
Tallis House
2 Tallis Street
London
EC4Y 0AB

Printed in Great Britain

Dedication

To George Speck, a mastermind that bettered the collective gastronomic experience of millions, may he rest in peace. To the Stray Kids of STAYville and to the Pirate Kings of Atiny Land, my source of joy and inspiration.

Acknowledgements

My thanks to my family, my parents and my sisters, for supporting me in this journey and in life. Thank you to Joseph M., my closest friend who has been the first person to ever read my book. I'll never thank you enough for always being there and encouraging me. Thank you Rawa G. for bringing to life my sketches and turning them into this amazing cover illustration. I would also like to thank the Olympia Publishers team for their work, and mostly my production coordinator Kristina Smith. Thank you to the designers, the editors, and the publicity team.

I would also like to acknowledge all the people who inspired me in so many different ways while I was writing these poems: my thanks to Bang Chan, Park Seonghwa, Lee Minho, Kim Hongjoong, Jeong Yunho, Kang Yeosang, Choi San, Song Mingi, Jung Wooyoung, Seo Changbin, Hwang Hyunjin, Han Jisung, Lee Felix, Kim Seungmin, Choi Jongho, and Yang Jeongin for inspiring me and giving me the motivation I needed to write this book through their music.

Thank you to Vishen Lakhiani for creating "The 6 Phase Meditation", this method is what enabled me to reach my dream of publishing my poems. And last but not least, I would like to thank Lisa Nichols, Natasha Graziano, and Tom Bilyeu. Their speeches gave me the courage to start.

Toward the night

Glancing at the mirror I saw a replication
Of what was far from imagination
My face, my smile, but not my eyes
Cold I was blue, covered in ice

I walked to the window,
From which moon could not be seen
As by clouds the sky was covered
Leaving the stars up there unseen,

I felt heavy as I climbed
But really light on the fall
As the sky I eyed
Going down the wall

And in the river, at the surface of water,
My reflection reached to me from underwater
Kept getting closer as the moon from me grew far
And from underwater, I might have seen the stars

Highway forest

I entered a forest
Of blue painted trees
I followed the steps
Left by the unseen
On the ground I saw
A broken piece of glass
Red fingerprints on the grass
Feathers of a bird
By the branches caged low

I kept walking ahead
As the road was leading me
To the river I came from

Now that back I was I saw
A white figure with deep dark eyes
On the muddy water floated
Shards of what once was a soul
The bright moon reflected

A hope

Butterflies fly in spring and summer
When the sun's shining high
And the weather is warmer
When there are flowers on the way
Even when they only live few days

I saw mine flying in a really dark place
Facing water and my back to the trees
Sitting with my arms hugging my knees
And my ghost wiping my tears away
Some decisions I once made
Today I deeply regret

Ninth bridge

All bridges go both ways
Some kind of bridges take you away
From a sad and lonely state
While some other kinds
Might just take you on a trip
To places you have never seen
Some kind of bridges are longer than others
Some of them take you to lonely places
I found silver branches adorning white blossoms
Lead white shining palaces
At the end of which deserted roads
And lonely shadows with cold painting trees

Kind company

In the darkest times
At the darkest places
During the darkest days
Darkness sometimes
Leads you away
It goes somewhere
To nowhere
Just far away
She asks you to stay
Promising to be by your side
She wishes you'll stay
And she'll keep you company
She's always there
When you feel so lonely
she's always there
when you walk a lonely road
she comes as fast and as soon as she knows
that nobody's here
and that no one knows
she doesn't want them back
and if back they come
she'll soon be gone

You have to know

life is a test
for the strong to stay
for the young to grow
for the old to go
and for the lonely to stray

On dried white roses

When it ends and everything comes back
When once blue skies now turned black
When hopes and dreams all come crashing down
And in a white dress, back on the ground

Souvenirs of a life that now is long gone
Silver flowers necklace my neck adorns
At my fingers red colors roses through their thorns
Each pearl of the bracelet now rolled alone

Undying heaviness of heart

To the child that died because of me
I in so many ways wish I could go back to see
Through your eyes that now are blind
I wish to heal the scars left by the wounds
Of the battles I pushed you to fight in
I wish I could see you again and your soft skin
Ivory white pearls in a thread
Tied by a knot around your wrist
I could never forget the details of your smile
Yet I'm here stuck and scared to forget
How bright burned your candle
Before giving up to the emptiness
And how your heart faded under the cracks
Now I still am collecting shards of glass
And dust of your dreams
That you've never seen

Silent thoughts

I feel stuck, trapped and lost
I look at the dark sky and wonder
If the sun will still rise again
Time passes and I'm getting older
Will I make it and be stronger
Will I even survive to my next year
I feel trapped and tied by this fear
Of finding myself here every year
And every day I'm running out of time
The sand keeps filling the hourglass
And my heart breaks under the pressure
As if of glass it was made
I sit in the corner and watch them laugh
I wonder if they fear what I fear
I wonder if they're happy behind their smiles
They all got to sleep and alone I stay
Overthinking about waking the next day
I overthink and hope again tonight
That tomorrow morning I wouldn't open my eyes

The hopes

I hope,
That one day I'll look back to where I came from
To be proud of the person I've become
To look back at the road and smile
And feel happy about how far I've come

I hope,
That when I look up I'll see the blue sky
That after the rain I'll see the rainbow, not the clouds
That I'll be able to tell my story
And that delighted I will show my smile

I hope,
That I'll make it to my next birthday
That during the nights I'll see the stars
And that in the morning,
My sun will rise

Reminiscence

One day, I will be gone
So make sure to remember
All the beautiful days
When I was still around

One day you'll think of me
And see how high I rose
Smelling a perfume of roses
In a field of forget-me-nots

A brighter future than that

I once dreamt about the future
Not a bright future, rather a brighter one
In which people were happy and all smiles
Not the fake ones we see on the pages

I dreamt that I could go out without worrying my mom
That I might get hurt because I am a woman
In that future that is brighter
I didn't need to be a fighter
In order to be respected for who I am

In that future that is much brighter
People never ended their lives
Society was accepting of us all
And each of us could live their life

In that dream I had of that future
I didn't fear wearing what I wanted to wear
I didn't feel excluded for wearing too much
Nor did the girls feel bad about not wearing that much

I dreamt of a future where life was easy
Not owning a car was okay
And not having my house and its keys
Didn't make me less of a human for lacking money

If I was given a wish to make
It would be for this dream to come true
For us as humans to be safe
And for a world that sees deeper than the surface

You'll get to see

Funny to see how
When you start the race few are here

Mostly to say goodbye
And maybe to see you there

Funny how no one's ready to stick with you
When the road gets hard toward your goal

People like to tell you what you can't do
People like to discourage you

Yet the same people will come rushing toward you
Trying to shine with you when you reach your destination

Keep your goals big and your vision clear
The one who discouraged you will be the first to hear

Knowing that

Time like water flies
And life is filled with lies
The world is full of haters
Watching from the theatres

Telling the ambitious to give up
Making you want to stop
Telling you it's not right
Close to the sun you might die

They think they're better
Thinking they know the truth
They'll try to tame your flame
To keep you out of the frame

In life

Some fights are too hard to be fought alone
Sometimes life is so harsh that you want to quit
Some people like to leave when they see your struggle
Some others like to watch from a distance
As your world turns upside down
And when you lay still on the ground
Your ghosts come to surround you
You want to let go but you can't
The darkness gets darker when no one's around
But you just need to keep your head up one more time
Tomorrow is a new day and you'll be strong enough
To get up one more time and try

Dimmed light

It was spring and it was still the night
Lights turned off, and it all went to death
While I stood there my mind overflowing with thoughts
Overthinking every small detail of my life
Now gazing from my window, biting my nail
Wondering if the flowers will soon bloom
Tomorrow morning or in the afternoon
As long as I'll see it one day

They'll soon bloom and I'll see them one day
Nights are long but they give place to the day
Moon is sun's reflection but in a darker way
Winter was long but now spring took its place
My nights are still long but I'll soon see the day
The day when flowers bloom in every color and shape
A road between the flowers butterflies will create
The sun shines and forces the past away
And my restless nights vanish with the days

Signs to stay

In colors I paint worlds of words and stories to tell
By every stroke of my brush I'm adding the details
Of a world created in my imagination
The longer you'll look, the more you get questions

Pouring my heart illustrating marvellous tales
In which symbolized evil only entails
Of a rising sun and a hero to take hold of its key
Turn up the lock unveiling the unseen

Yesterday's caterpillars igniting the stars
Of a wandering spirit roaming the dark
Dimness of the heart roared alight
From the glass edifice hued the night

And if the candle's fire melted its wax
Making the cave smaller and dark
Light enters from the window's cracks
Showing you where left are the marks

Your road

Striving for immensity and magnitude in a location
Locking your life, and your dreams with limitations
Cause as contrasting the norms you shall not be seen
Doomed to spend an existence outside the scene

And if life is full of tracks and directions
Keep in mind that your destination
Even if different by no means is wrong
And that you don't always have to be strong

So go toward your goals and avoid regrets
Of what if you took another path in your quest
For if the other one you would have taken
The road you're on today you would believe was better

On ground

In a yellow field of carnations
Alone sitting on the grass and thinking
When morning goes and comes back
What is tomorrow going to be like

As of the flowing time I'm scared
And in the lonely times I feared
If a bird flies to my life
I would like me better I suppose

Uneasy

Sometimes I just want to give up on everything
Starting from my life and down to my dreams
Sometimes I just want to go back to how I used to feel
I want to be able to sleep without the crushing weight
Of the pressure of my goals and dreams
Heavy on my heart as I try to sleep
And insomnia comes and won't let me get away
Bringing anxiety along and nothing's okay
I feel as if I failed but I only started last year
And the lack of outcome makes me tremble in fear
Fearing that my efforts will just vanish with time
And that from the future I'll look at me now and say
That if more efforts I gave it would have been okay
That it is my fault for staying behind
And I am the one in the wrong for aiming too high
Awake I stay in my bed for the longest hours
Wondering when did everything go wrong
When did I become a coward scared of facing my fears
People my age and younger are up ahead of me
And it's like sitting in station twenty-one waiting for your train to come
Every year your station's number gets higher with no outcome
But all I see is people coming after and going before
And alone I sit as lights are turned off

My aim isn't even that big to start with
People achieved better with less efforts
And I wait and wait and wait but to no avail
And when I look at the past me I feel so bad
For being a failure and not being enough
what scares me the most is giving up on this dream
And having my future self watch my lonely self of now
And tell me that if I had just tried one more time
Stayed up one more night
We would have today found ourselves in better places

Mind telling stories of a future

It started with a dream
Of us two, walking side by side
A garden of white flowers at our right
And one six on that yellow shirt's back

We walked on that circular road
By the end of which we took a new turn
One seven now after six years of teens
In the garden dogs played as we walked around

At my left I saw my childhood friend
Standing, yellow veils in both hands
As I passed my friend's back was what to me is turned
Now on a bike I was as continued the dream

On the third turn I fell from the bike
Hair longer with now one eight on the back
Three brown dogs attacked me
As I tried hiding under a lemon tree

On a horseback that one came to me
Taking my hand and me from the hiding
I got up and we made one more turn
One stayed but eight to nine changed

I do not recall all of the dream
Fifteen to twenty one was a long way to me
But memories I recall is at two zero I fell
That person's dream continued without me

All that is

When we parted and I felt the world end
White turned black and even
My sun stopped shining leaving me cold in the dark
As that was the illusion I rotate around

I had it all one day
And by leaving, I lost it all
I lost my smile, my light, and my reason to live
With no further words my dream disappeared

I reached out but there was no solution
I was sitting down crying in confusion
Wiping my tears and your light close to my heart
But like a candle, the light dimmed with time

If by missing, you could bring back what you've lost
I would have never lost that dream in the first place
And everytime I thought of this place
Another breakdown I would face

Cold floor under me as I sat on the ground
I wished to find the light somewhere close to me
And my sleepless nights would bring no dreams
Yet I wanted to put myself to sleep, and never open my eyes

I thought about what went wrong in between the lines
But this place was what was wrong
Like matching pieces of puzzle we thought
That the world enjoyed keeping apart

And if I sleep you're the dream that haunts my dreams
Versions of a life created in other realms
Cause we've never been that close to be
Or did I just want the blame on this world to be

After years, I still hold onto the memories
I still dream of the past when I manage to sleep
And maybe that's my way for healing the wounds
But how much time is needed from me to stay to heal

As your moon only reflecting you in the night
I had no more my safe place to be
And what equals years spent from my life
The same number in days it took us to part"

Dedicated path

The streets were empty
And the road stood lonely
As in the dark I stumbled blindly
Leaving the ghosts behind me

Why is the path so desolated
When I chose to make it my way
In the cold I felt isolated
The vision getting blurred ahead

No street lights kept it illuminated
As a moth to the flame I gravitated
The conditions made it hard to stay
Yet forward I kept walking on my way

The darker my world became
My feet wavering on the ground
And with no other source of light
Eight stars shone alive

View of hopes and a better life
That I have never seen in the past
The road was still long ahead
But didn't seem as hard as before

Earning

Sometimes it just is a little light that brings you hope
A word and a smile is what keeps you alive

And you just need to know that you're not alone
Sometimes it's just the stars that lit your dark skies

When you were on your blurry and lonely road
Similar to a candle that lights and warms your home

Tears long forgotten as now of joy you cry
Hardships now gone that they're left behind

Blinded by the night under a new light you see
How great it feels when you reach your dreams

Matter of fact

Today, as yesterday and as long as the past
The memories of the days I felt happiness that lasts
I feel numb and cold and I feel the sharp edges
I still hear the sounds of a heart that shatters

I feel empty, deserted, housing orphan pieces of my heart
Abandoned and lonely, the memories tearing me apart
They ask how I feel, and only hear the words
Yet if they look in my eyes, they would've seen the wounds

Elsetime

The nights get colder
And I'm getting older
And time passes by
But still I try to hold on

I see my face
And I ask myself
That dream I want
Will I realize?

I see mountains of doubts
That I have to climb
That I have to defeat
And then come my scars

She whispers in my ear
In her honey voice
Reminder of my fears
And my tears, and I fall

She says, let go
Forget your dreams
It's not meant to be real
Can't you see the signs

She says, you can't enter battles
You're not sure you'll win
You can't waste your time
On what is only a dream

Yet when I weaken
And I start to loosen my grip
She laughs at me and watches
As I fall in, deep

I then become scared
Of failure and defeat
And in this world obscured
No lights shine down here

No dreams seem close
No goals seem right
Under the shadow of light
Stars can't shine bright

I feel the cold
Seeping in my bones
Crawling to my heart
And clutching my throat

As if to ask me why
Did I stay here
Why am I trapped
Caught like a deer

But then sometimes

Darkness let you see through
Lessens the shadows
Some lights approach you

It is always unexpected
Always surprising
But not less than true
With hope it ignites

Gives you sight
Of dreams to come to life
Of dreams waiting for you
So you can get it through

So never lose hope
Cause in the darkest times
There will be light
That brightens your life

Sometimes it comes from stars
And sometimes it comes from beyond
But never forget that the brightest flames
Come from within the hearts

Scars and starry skies

Life is easy they say,
But they never tell you,
About how hard it becomes,
When they all leave you,

They just disappear
With no warning sign
Without a goodbye
Their ghosts lingering behind

It's funny how they leave
When you need them the most
All the ones you loved
Only remain the ghosts

You can't see the road
It seems so dark
No light is here
To illuminate your path

But never lose hope
You will find your stars
They will lead you to the moon
And brighten your skies

Shooting stars travel
During the darkest nights

To see and to save

When you see the rainbow
In hues of gray
When you say you're fine
But you're not okay
When your smile is wide
But you're fading away
When you look in the mirror
And don't see yourself

I know that feeling
I understand the pain
Cause I held my hand
When no one was around
I learned to wear my mask
I felt the pain
I know the feeling
Of fading away

I felt it all
I went through it
I was all alone
Nobody knew it
I wiped my tears
And broke my fears

And as I hugged myself
Through the loneliness
I was the one who saved myself

Another season

People come in your life
Like the start of a new season,
But they won't stay for long
When it turns to the next season,

Some of them hold onto you,
Like a leaf to the branch,
Holding onto you despite the cold
Scared of falling and losing you,

Some will leave and go,
As fast as time goes,
When it gets tricky and cold,
They go back to their homes

From your life they disappear,
Only the memories remain,
As time passes, people change,
Memories stay to mend your pain

And I keep in the moments
To cherish and keep safe
One day we'll all be gone
Even if now they leave,
It will be okay

Yards of lilies

I now expect her visits
As soon as down I start feeling
She comes to hold my hand
When I'm left behind

She tells me that I am alone
Cause I am not a loved person
She says that they left
Cause they care for others more

She then shows me my room
And describe its emptiness
Which makes me drown more
In my dark loneliness

Then she smiles and hold my face
Her cold fingers freezing my skin
She reassures me that She, will always stay
As long as I am alone

Eight

I have once received a gift
From the one whom to me was dear
A silver chain delicate and fragile
The white metal light as air

It adorned my wrist
With three infinity signs
Small diamonds shining
Like the night's bright stars

Things went down
And the bracelet broke
Losing an eight out of three
The two others alone

To say that an eight I lost
The two others I found
Or by them I was found
When at my lowest I stood

What felt like missing pieces
Of my hearts were back
Silver chains once white
Now of poison turned black